21st Century Junior Library

PLANTS WE WEAR

by Pam Rosenberg

CHERRY LAKE PUBLISHING * ANN ARBOR, MICHIGAN

Published in the United States of America by Cherry Lake Publishing
Ann Arbor, Michigan
www.cherrylakepublishing.com

Content Adviser: Paul Young, MA, Botanist

Reading Consultant: Cecilia Minden-Cupp, PhD, Literacy Specialist and Author

Photo Credits: Cover and page 4, ©iStockphoto.com/knape; cover and page 6, ©Jerry Horbert, used under license from Shutterstock, Inc.; page 8, ©iStockphoto.com/kaupo; page 10, ©iStockphoto.com/danishkhan; cover and page 12, ©iStockphoto.com/WinterWitch; page 14, ©zhu difeng, used under license from Shutterstock, Inc.; cover and page 16, ©Doxa, used under license from Shutterstock, Inc.; page 18, ©Stuart Taylor, used under license from Shutterstock, Inc.; page 20, ©Corbis Super RF/Alamy

LIBRARY OF CONGRESS CATALOGING-IN-PUBLICATION DATA
Rosenberg, Pam.
  Plants we wear / by Pam Rosenberg.
     p. cm.—(21st century junior library)
  Includes bibliographical references and index.
  ISBN-13: 978-1-60279-277-7
  ISBN-10: 1-60279-277-1
  1. Plants, Useful—Study and teaching (Elementary) I. Title. II. Series.
  QK98.4.A1R67 2008
  581.6'3—dc22   2008011347

Cherry Lake Publishing would like to acknowledge the work of
The Partnership for 21st Century Skills.
Please visit www.21stcenturyskills.org for more information.

CONTENTS

5 Look at the Label

7 Cotton Plants

13 Other Plants We Wear

17 From Head to Toe

22 Glossary

23 Find Out More

24 Index

24 About the Author

Most clothes have labels that tell you what they are made of.

Look at the Label

Do you wear jeans? A lot of people do. Look inside your favorite pair of jeans. Does it say they are made of cotton?

Cotton is just one plant we use to make clothes. There are many others. People have been using parts of plants to make cloth for **thousands** of years. Let's take a look at some plants we wear.

Cotton bolls open up when the cotton is almost ready to be picked.

Cotton Plants

Have you ever seen a cotton plant? Cotton plants have woody **stems**. The plants grow flowers. Then the flowers fall off and leave **bolls** behind. The bolls have seeds inside.

Make a Guess!

How many of your family's shirts are made of cotton? Find 10 shirts, but don't look at the labels. Guess how many of the shirts are made from cotton. Write down the number. Now take a look at the labels. Was your guess correct?

It takes a lot of cotton to make a bale.

White **fibers** grow from the seeds. The boll cracks open when the ball of fibers gets big. Then you can see the fluffy white fibers. The cotton fibers will soon be ready for **harvest**.

The cotton fibers are picked. Then they are separated from the seeds using a machine called a **cotton gin**. They are cleaned and pressed into large bundles called **bales**.

Cotton is turned into yarn in a textile mill.

The bales of cotton are shipped to **textile** mills. Textile mills are factories that turn cotton into **yarn**. Then the yarn is made into cloth. The cloth is shipped to factories that make clothes. Workers in those factories will turn the cotton cloth into T-shirts, jeans, and other things.

Think!

Can you think of something that is made of cotton that you don't wear? Hint: You probably sleep on them at night.
Did you say sheets? If you did, you are correct. Many sheets that we use on beds are made from cotton.

Fibers from flax plants are used to make linen cloth.

Other Plants We Wear

Some clothes are made from a cloth called **linen**. Linen is made from the fibers of **flax** plants. Flax plants have tall stems and blue flowers. The fibers used to make linen come from the stems of the plants. Linen fibers are very strong and smooth.

Have you ever seen a bamboo plant? Maybe you know that pandas eat bamboo.

Some kinds of bamboo can grow to be more than 100 feet (30 meters) tall.

But bamboo isn't just for pandas. Some kinds of bamboo plants are used to make cloth.

Bamboo is a tall grass. It grows very quickly. The fibers in its long stems can be made into yarn. The yarn is made into cloth. Then the cloth can be made into all kinds of things we wear.

Look!

Look around your house for things made of cloth. Some things to look for are clothes, towels, sheets, and stuffed animals. Look at the labels. Write down the name of each item and what it is made of. Were any of them made of cotton, linen, or bamboo?

The stalks of wheat plants can be used to make hats. The seeds are used for food.

From Head to Toe

Have you ever seen a straw hat? Straw hats can be made from the leaves of palm trees. They can also be made from the stalks of grain plants such as wheat and oats. The seeds of the grain plants are used for food. The dried stalks can be woven into straw hats.

Latex drips from a cut in a rubber tree.

What do plants have to do with athletic shoes? Some of the material in the soles of your shoes may come from rubber trees. Rubber trees have a milky liquid called **latex**.

Workers make cuts in the bark of rubber trees. Then the latex oozes out and is collected in containers. The latex is made into rubber. The rubber can be used to make shoes and other products.

Take a look around your classroom. How many kids are wearing plants?

So take a look in your closet. Check out the labels. See if you can dress from head to toe in plants you wear!

Ask Questions!

Librarians are good at helping people find facts. Ask your librarian to help you find more information about cotton, flax, and bamboo plants. Want to know more about straw or rubber? Just ask!

21

GLOSSARY

bales (BAYLZ) large bundles of things such as cotton or hay

bolls (BOHLS) the parts of cotton plants that hold the seeds

cotton gin (KOT-uhn JIN) a machine that separates the seeds from cotton fibers

fibers (FYE-burz) long, thin, tough threads of something

flax (FLAX) a plant with blue flowers that produces fibers that can be made into linen

harvest (HAR-vist) the gathering of crops that are ready for use

latex (LAY-tex) a milky liquid that comes from certain plants and is used to make rubber

librarians (lye-BRAR-ee-uhnz) people who work in libraries and help people find books and information

linen (LIN-uhn) cloth that is made from the fibers of the flax plant

stems (STEMZ) the long parts of plants from which leaves and flowers grow

textile (TEK-stile) a cloth that has been woven or knitted from yarn or thread

thousands (THOU-suhndz) more than one group of 1,000; one thousand is 10 groups of 100

yarn (YARN) fibers that have been twisted or spun into long strands for weaving or knitting cloth

FIND OUT MORE

BOOKS

Mitchell, Melanie. *Cloth.* Minneapolis: Lerner, 2003.

Oxlade, Chris. *How We Use Cotton.* Chicago: Raintree, 2004.

WEB SITES

Cotton's Journey— Watch Cotton Grow

www.cottonsjourney.com/ watchcotton/default.asp
Look at pictures that show cotton plants from seedlings to harvest

Kid Zone—Rubber Tree

www.wildernessclassroom.com/ students/archives/2005/03/ rubber_tree.html
Read more about rubber trees

INDEX

B
bales, 9, 11
bamboo, 13, 15, 21
bark, 19
bolls, 7, 9

C
cloth, 5, 11, 13, 15
cotton, 5, 7, 9, 11,
   15, 21
cotton gins, 9

F
factories, 11
fibers, 9, 13, 15
flax plants, 13, 21
flowers, 7, 13
foods, 17

G
grains, 17
grass, 15

H
harvest, 9

J
jeans, 5, 11

L
labels, 7, 15, 21
latex, 19
leaves, 17
librarians, 21
linen, 13, 15

O
oats, 17

P
palm trees, 17
pandas, 13, 15

Q
questions, 21

R
rubber trees, 19, 21

S
seeds, 7, 9, 17
sheets, 11, 15
shirts, 7, 11
shoes, 19
stalks, 17
stems, 7, 13, 15
straw hats, 17, 21
stuffed animals, 15

T
textile mills, 11
towels, 15
trees, 17, 19

W
weaving, 17
wheat, 17

Y
yarn, 11, 15

ABOUT THE AUTHOR

Pam Rosenberg is a former teacher who currently works as a writer and editor of children's books. She lives in Arlington Heights, Illinois.